JUL 2007

W9-CPJ-471

Usborne

Starting Fishing

Fiona Patchett

Designed by Rachel Kirkland and Jan McCafferty

Illustrated by Joanna Venus, Kevin Lyles
and Chris Shields

Edited by Kamini Khanduri and Felicity Brooks
Photographs by Howard Allman
Consultant: Dr. Bruno Broughton
Cover design by Neil Francis

Contents

About fishing

Fishing, or angling, is one of the oldest sports in the world. There are lots of ways to catch fish. This book shows you two of the most popular ones – float fishing and leger fishing and how to put fish back in the water without harming them.

Tackle

To go fishing, you need some basic equipment called tackle. Most of it is fairly cheap to buy in fishing stores, but you can learn how to make some of it in this book. This picture shows the tackle you need for float fishing.

You use a landing net to lift the fish out of the water after you have caught it.

The rod lets you hold the line over the water.

The reel lets you wind the line in and out of the water.

Float fishing

Float fishing is fishing with a float and split shot (little weights) on your line. It is the best way to catch fish that swim near the surface. You can use it in water that is still or flowing, but not too rough.

Leger fishing

Leger fishing is fishing with a weight but no float. It is best for catching fish that swim near the bottom of the water. It is good in rough water too, because the weight keeps the bait in one place.

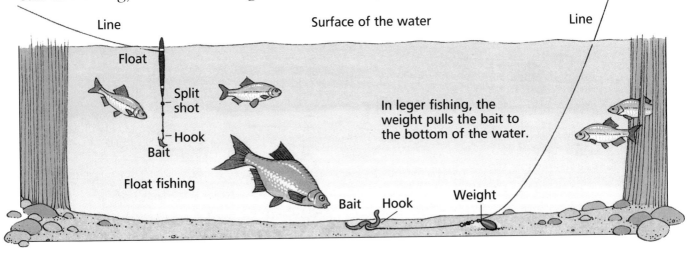

Line

Surface of the water

Line

Float

Split shot

Hook

Bait

Float fishing

In leger fishing, the weight pulls the bait to the bottom of the water.

Bait   Hook   Weight

*For a link to a website where you can shade in pictures of fish, try quizzes and find out lots of fishy facts, go to **www.usborne-quicklinks.com***

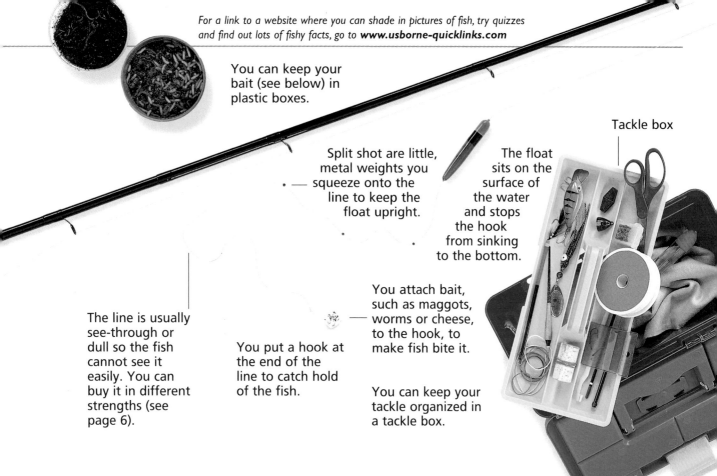

You can keep your bait (see below) in plastic boxes.

Tackle box

Split shot are little, metal weights you squeeze onto the line to keep the float upright.

The float sits on the surface of the water and stops the hook from sinking to the bottom.

The line is usually see-through or dull so the fish cannot see it easily. You can buy it in different strengths (see page 6).

You put a hook at the end of the line to catch hold of the fish.

You attach bait, such as maggots, worms or cheese, to the hook, to make fish bite it.

You can keep your tackle organized in a tackle box.

Salt water and fresh water

Different kinds of fish live in different types of water. The two main types of water are salt water and fresh water.

Be careful if the waves are high.

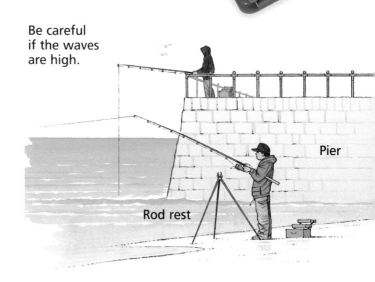

Pier

Rod rest

Fresh water is water that is not salty. In rivers, streams and canals, it flows. In ponds and lakes, it is still. Find out about freshwater fish on page 28.

The water in or near seas and oceans is called salt water. You can fish in salt water from a pier or from a beach. Find out about saltwater fish on page 29.

3

Before you go

Before you set off on a fishing trip, you need to think about where and when to go. Fish are most likely to eat your bait early in the morning or after it has rained, so these are good times to go.

Things to take

You also need to think of all the things you might need to take. You won't enjoy fishing if you are wet, hungry, too hot or too cold. Here are some things you should remember to take with you.

Permission to fish

Ask in a tackle store where you are allowed to fish. You might need to buy a permit to fish in your chosen spot. There are also certain times of the year, called closed seasons, when you are not allowed to catch fish because they are laying eggs.

FISHING PERMIT

Take a cap with a brim and polarized sunglasses to help you see in bright sunlight.

Remember to take some food and drink with you.

Sunscreen stops your skin from burning.

A container to hold your money

A cloth to clean tackle

A watch so you know how long you have been out

A whistle to attract attention if you need help

Take a notebook, pens and weighing scales (from a tackle store) to make records of the fish you catch. See pages 24-25.

Where to fish

When you arrive at the waterside, look for a safe spot to stand. Try to find a place where there are plenty of fish. Anglers learn where to find fish by looking for clues in the water. This is called 'reading the water'. Here are some of the places you may find fish.

Waterside safety

- Always take someone with you when you go fishing.
- Learn to swim.
- Tell an adult where you are going and when you will be back.
- Before you fish near the sea, check in a tackle store what time the tide comes in. Be careful fishing then.
- Never fish near overhead wires. The electricity can travel down your rod if it goes near them.
- Always fish from a place where the ground is firm and keep well back from the edge of the water.

Some fish live in fast-flowing water, for example, near waterfalls.

You can often find fish in the shady water under overhanging trees and shrubs.

You can usually find fish where there are insects.

Many fish swim in these swirls, called eddies.

Some fish swim near reeds.

Many fish live in quiet, still pools.

Fish often look for food near piers or moored boats.

Small bubbles on the surface of the water can mean that fish are feeding below.

5

Making a rod

This page tells you how to make your own fishing rod out of a bamboo cane. You can use it to catch small fish.

You will need: a bamboo cane about 3m (10ft) long; 3m (10ft) of fishing line; a cork; a barbless hook (see below); a rubber band.

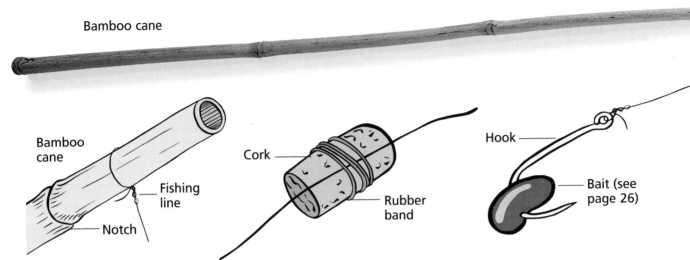

Bamboo cane

Bamboo cane

Fishing line

Notch

Cork

Rubber band

Hook

Bait (see page 26)

1. Tie the fishing line just above the last notch of the bamboo cane with a half-blood knot (see page 10).

2. Wrap the rubber band around the cork and line, 2m (6ft) away from the end of the bamboo cane.

3. Tie a hook to the end of the line with a half-blood knot. Before you use the rod, add some bait.

Hooks, baits and line

Some hooks have a barb which makes them difficult to remove from a fish's mouth. Make sure you buy a barbless hook (a hook without a barb) so you can remove it without damaging the fish.

Hold the line above the hook so you don't hurt yourself.

This hook has a barb. Always buy barbless hooks.

Fishing line comes in different strengths. In fresh water, the best strengths to use are 1.5kg (3.2lb) line for float fishing and 3.2kg (6lb) for leger fishing.

Most foods make good bait, so try out a few different kinds. Find out more about baits on page 26.

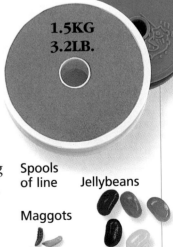

1.5KG 3.2LB.

Spools of line

Jellybeans

Maggots

Cheese

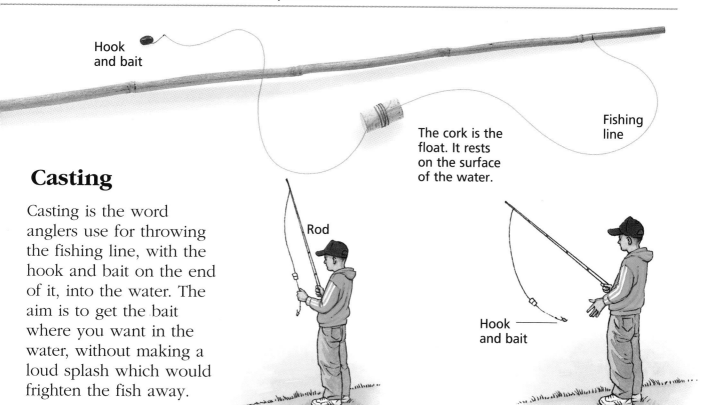

Hook and bait

The cork is the float. It rests on the surface of the water.

Fishing line

Rod

Hook and bait

Casting

Casting is the word anglers use for throwing the fishing line, with the hook and bait on the end of it, into the water. The aim is to get the bait where you want in the water, without making a loud splash which would frighten the fish away.

This is how you cast with a home-made rod. You can learn about different ways of casting with a rod and reel later in the book.

1. Hold your rod with one hand. Hold the end of the line, above the hook and bait, with your other hand. Then tip the rod forward.

2. Let go of the line so that it swings out over the water. When the bait has hit the water, hold the rod in both hands.

Casting tips

Try to stand with the sun facing you when you cast, so your shadow doesn't fall on the water and scare the fish away. Fish have very good hearing and will swim off if you stamp around or make too much noise.

Cork floats on the surface of the water.

3. If you see the cork go underwater, a fish is biting your bait. You can find out how to get your fish out of the water on page 23.

Rods, reels and line

If you want to catch bigger fish, you will need to buy a proper rod and reel from a tackle store. These pages show you how to fix together a rod and how to attach the reel and line.

Putting the rod together

You buy rods in two or three sections. Rods can be very long when you put them together, so make sure you have plenty of space.

Middle section

Butt

Tip

Middle section

1. Push the butt into the middle section as far as it will go. Then push the middle section into the tip.

2. Twist the sections around until all the rod rings are on the same side of the rod.

The reel

You fit the foot of the reel into the reel fittings on the rod handle. You can fix the reel handle to either side of the reel, depending on whether you are left or right-handed.

Spool

Spool lip

This lever is called the bale arm. It stops the line from slipping off the reel.

The line slides over this groove, called a roller.

Foot

Reel handle

Rods often come in three sections.

Middle section

The butt is the thickest section of the rod.

The tip is the thinnest section.

The line passes through these rod rings.

The rod handle is part of the butt.

The reel fits into these reel fittings.

This button can stop you from winding line off the reel.

Tighten this screw to stop too much line from coming off the reel.

Attaching the reel and line

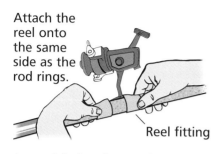

Attach the reel onto the same side as the rod rings.

Reel fitting

1. Hold the foot of the reel between the reel fittings on the rod, with the spool facing the rod tip. Slide the reel fittings over the foot.

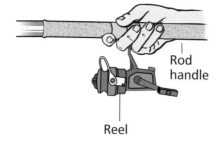

Rod handle

Reel

2. Hold the rod in one hand so the rod tip points away from you. The reel and rod rings should be nearest to the ground.

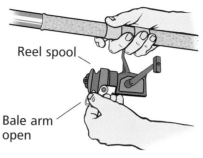

Reel spool

Bale arm open

3. Open the bale arm by pulling it over the end of the spool so that it points to the rod tip. Now you can add the line.

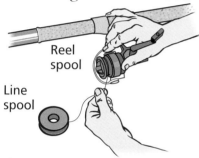

Reel spool

Line spool

4. Unwind about 1m (3ft) of line. Tie the end to the reel spool with any knot. Wrap the line around a few times until it stays in place.

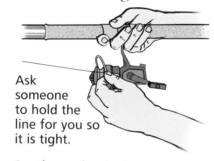

Ask someone to hold the line for you so it is tight.

5. Close the bale arm by snapping it back over the end of the reel spool. This stops the line from coming off the spool.

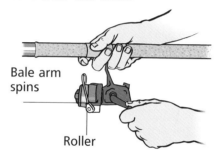

Bale arm spins

Roller

6. Turn the reel handle away from you to make the bale arm spin. Keep the line tight so the line slides over the roller, onto the spool.

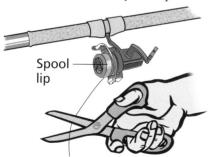

Spool lip

7. Keep turning the reel handle until the line reaches the spool lip. Then cut the line about 10cm (25in) from the reel.

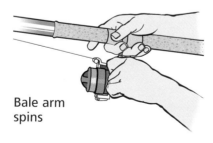

Bale arm spins

8. To wind line off the reel, turn the reel handle toward you. Pull the line away from you and thread it through all the rod rings.

9. You can find out how to add a hook on pages 10-11, the bait on page 26, float tackle on page 14 and leger tackle on page 18.

Knots

These are some of the knots you need to know how to tie. You can use them for attaching tackle to your line.

Half-blood knot

Half-blood knots are very useful. You can use them to tie your line to a hook, a bamboo cane to make your own rod or various other items of tackle. This is how you tie a half-blood knot to a hook.

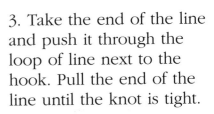

Simple loop knot

Half-blood knot

Loop to loop knot

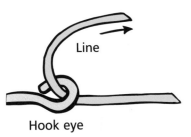

Line

Hook eye

1. Hold the end of the line in one hand and the hook in the other. Thread about 6cm (2in) of the line through the hook eye.

Make four loops around the line.

2. Hold the eye of the hook with one hand. Twist the end of the line around the line on the other side of the hook eye four times.

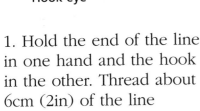

Pull this line until the knot is tight, then cut it off near the knot.

3. Take the end of the line and push it through the loop of line next to the hook. Pull the end of the line until the knot is tight.

Simple loop knot

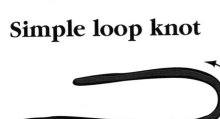

◄——— 10cm (6in) ———►

1. Fold a piece of line back so it is double for about 10cm (6in). Hold the double line at each end.

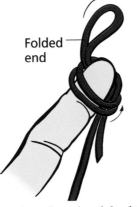

Folded end

2. Make the double line into a loose circle around your first finger and push the folded end through it.

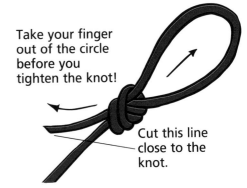

Take your finger out of the circle before you tighten the knot!

Cut this line close to the knot.

3. Pull the folded end one way and the line on the other side of the circle the other to tighten the knot.

Hook lengths

A hook length is a short piece of line with a hook tied to one end and a simple loop knot at the other. You can attach one to the reel line with a loop to loop knot (see below). Loop to loop knots are easy to take apart, so if your hook breaks you can replace the whole hook length quickly. Here's how you make a hook length.

Practice

It can be difficult to tie knots with fishing line because it is slippery. It is a good idea to try tying these knots with string before you use line.

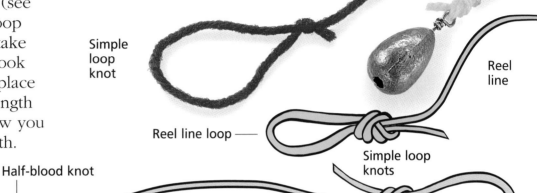

Loop to loop knot

Simple loop knot

Half-blood knot

Reel line loop

Reel line

Simple loop knots

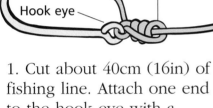

Half-blood knot

Hook eye

Hook length

1. Cut about 40cm (16in) of fishing line. Attach one end to the hook eye with a half-blood knot. Do not touch the hook point.

2. Make a simple loop knot at the other end of the hook length. Make a few hook lengths so you have some spares.

3. Tie a simple loop knot at the end of the reel line. You can then attach the hook length with a loop to loop knot.

Loop to loop knot

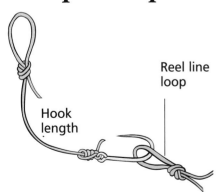

Reel line loop

Hook length

1. Push the hook at the end of the hook length through the reel line loop.

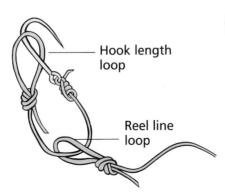

Hook length loop

Reel line loop

2. Push the hook through the loop at the end of the hook length.

Be very careful not to hurt yourself on the hook as you pull.

3. Pull the hook one way and the reel line the other to tighten the knot.

11

Underarm casting

There are two ways to cast with a rod and reel: underarm and overhead. Underarm casting is the best if you want to catch fish that swim close to the edge of the water. You can learn about overhead casting on pages 20-21.

Underarm casting doesn't take up too much space, so it is good if there are trees and bushes around.

Hold the rod by its handle, with your hand around the foot of the reel when you cast.

Hold the rod almost upright as you cast.

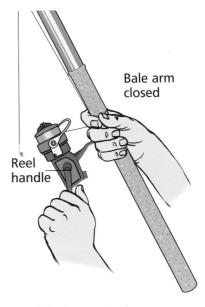

Bale arm closed

Reel handle

1. Hold the rod almost upright in one hand. Turn the reel handle with the other hand, until the hook and bait reach the reel.

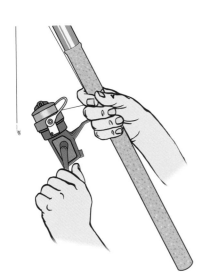

2. Press the line coming off the reel against the rod handle with the first finger of the hand holding the rod, as shown here.

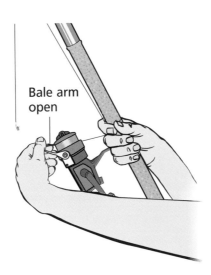

Bale arm open

3. Open the bale arm by pulling it over the spool. The line will not come off the reel because you are holding it with your finger.

4. Hold the end of the line with your other hand, just above the hook and bait. Be careful not to hurt yourself on the hook.

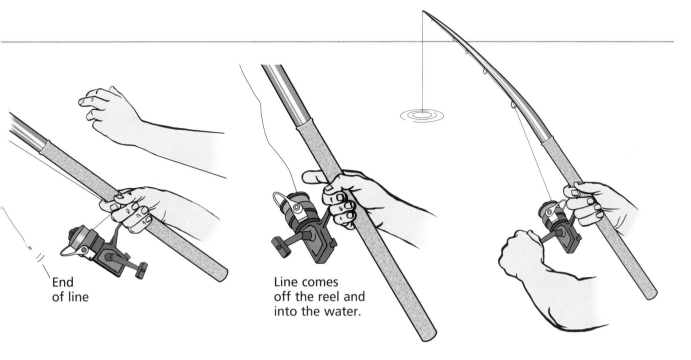

End of line

Line comes off the reel and into the water.

5. Tip the rod forward slightly. Let go of the line so it swings out over the water. Keep your finger pressed against the rod.

6. As the line swings over the water, lift your finger off the line held against the rod handle. This lets more line off the reel.

7. When the bait hits the water, turn the reel handle away from you, so the bale arm closes and the line tightens.

Casting game

You need four pieces of rope about 2m (6ft) long. (You can buy rope from a hardware store.) Lay one piece in a straight line on the ground. Lay the others in circles at various distances from it. Stand behind the straight piece and cast your line. The goal is to get your line into a circle.

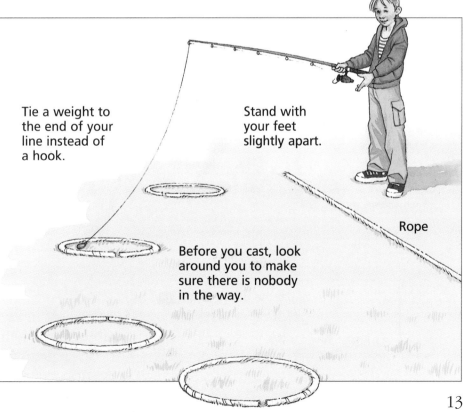

Tie a weight to the end of your line instead of a hook.

Stand with your feet slightly apart.

Before you cast, look around you to make sure there is nobody in the way.

Rope

13

Float fishing

Float fishing is a very good way to catch fish in water that is shallow, muddy, weedy or rocky. When you have put your rod, reel and line together, you attach a float and split shot to the line. These hold the bait at the right depth in the water. The float also shows you when a fish bites your bait (see the section on striking on the opposite page).

This picture shows a float and split shot attached to a line.

The top of the float is bright so you can see it from far away.

You use a float ring to attach the float to the line.

The part that goes underwater is dull so it doesn't frighten fish away.

This is a loop to loop knot (see page 11).

Split shot have little slits in them so you can squeeze them on the line easily.

—Hook length

Float eye

The split shot weigh down the bait and make the float sit upright in the water.

Barbless hook

Attaching a float and split shot

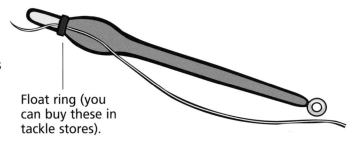

Float ring (you can buy these in tackle stores).

1. Slide a float ring onto the line, about 1m (3ft) from the end. Push the bright end of the float through the float ring so it points to the rod.

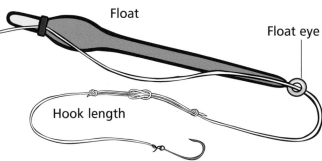

Float

Float eye

Hook length

2. Thread the line through the float eye. If the float doesn't have an eye, use another float ring instead. Then tie a hook length (see page 11) to the end of the line.

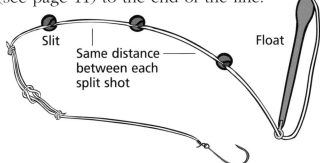

Slit

Same distance between each split shot

Float

3. After you have set the float in the right position (see 'setting the float' opposite), you can squeeze on about three or four split shot, between the float and the hook.

For a link to a website where you can find out many fascinating facts about fish, go to www.usborne-quicklinks.com

Setting the float

Before you attach the split shot and bait, you have to make sure that the float is in the right position in the water and that the bait will hang above the bottom. To find out how deep the water is, attach a plummet (see below) to the line and cast it into the water.

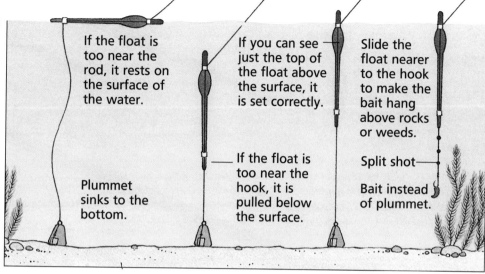

If the float is too near the rod, it rests on the surface of the water.

Plummet sinks to the bottom.

If you can see just the top of the float above the surface, it is set correctly.

If the float is too near the hook, it is pulled below the surface.

Slide the float nearer to the hook to make the bait hang above rocks or weeds.

Split shot

Bait instead of plummet.

You can buy a plummet from a tackle store. Thread the line through the ring on the top. Push the hook into the cork strip.

This float is set too near the rod. Wind the line out of the water. Slide the float down the line and cast again.

This float is set too near the hook. Wind the line out of the water. Slide the float up the line and cast again.

These floats are set correctly. The float sits upright and you can just see the top above the surface of the water.

Striking

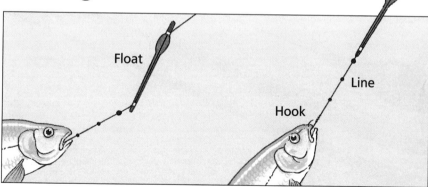

Float

Line

Hook

1. Watch your float carefully on the surface of the water. You can tell when a fish bites your bait because the float wobbles around or disappears underwater.

2. When a fish bites the bait, lift the tip of your rod quickly upward. The line tightens and the hook goes into the fish's mouth. This is called striking.

3. If you don't feel a fish taking your bait after a few minutes, cast again. It may help to try out different baits or to move to a new patch of water.

15

Different floats

Floats come in lots of shapes and sizes that you can use in different types of water. Here are a few you can try out. The opposite page shows you how to make a float out of a drinking straw. Perhaps you can think up some other ways of making floats.

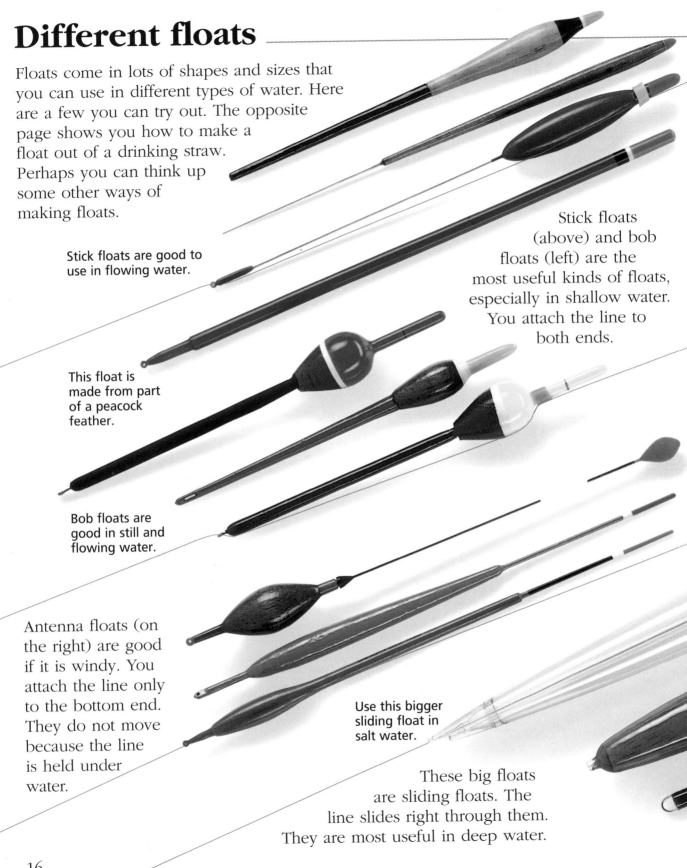

Stick floats are good to use in flowing water.

This float is made from part of a peacock feather.

Bob floats are good in still and flowing water.

Stick floats (above) and bob floats (left) are the most useful kinds of floats, especially in shallow water. You attach the line to both ends.

Antenna floats (on the right) are good if it is windy. You attach the line only to the bottom end. They do not move because the line is held under water.

Use this bigger sliding float in salt water.

These big floats are sliding floats. The line slides right through them. They are most useful in deep water.

Drinking straw float

You can use this drinking straw float to catch little fish that swim in still water. Remember to let the paint and glue dry before you try it out in the water.

You will need:

1 bright, plastic drinking straw; waterproof glue; rubber float ring; paper clip; strong thread; a paintbrush; 1 pot of waterproof paint in a dull shade.

1. Paint two thirds of the plastic drinking straw in a dull shade. You should leave the other third of the straw bright.

Straw

Put a little glue into an old saucer.

2. Wait for the paint to dry. Dip each end of the straw in some glue. Make sure both ends are filled so no water can get in.

When you use a sliding float, tie a knot close to the reel. When the knot reaches the float, it stops more line from going into the water.

Paper clip

Straw

3. Before the glue dries, push a paper clip into the the dull end of the straw. Make sure one end sticks out to make a loop.

Line

Rubber float ring

4. When the glue is dry, slide a float ring up the line. Push the bright end of the straw through it to hold the straw against the line.

Thread the line through the paper clip loop.

5. Pull more line through the float ring and thread it through the paper clip loop. Attach any more tackle to the end of the line.

Drinking straw floats

17

Leger fishing

If you want to catch bigger fish and fish that feed at the bottom of deep water, you need to take the float and split shot off the line and attach a heavier weight, called a leger weight, instead. You can cast this tackle into the water, either underarm or overhead.

This picture shows a kind of leger weight and a swivel attached to a line.

Leger weights pull the hook and bait to the bottom of the water.

Leger weights help you to cast farther. They also hold the bait still in rough or fast-flowing water.

This is a swivel. It is used to stop the weight from sliding down to the hook. It also stops the line from twisting.

Loop to loop knot (see page 11)

Hook

How to attach a weight and swivel to your line

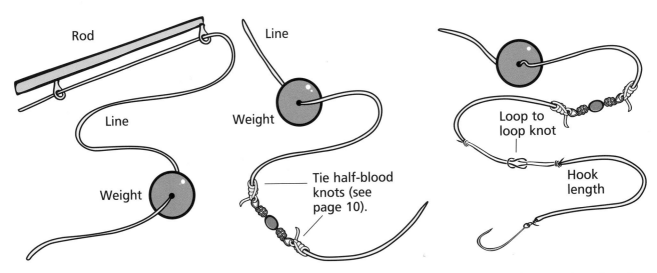

Rod

Line

Line

Weight

Weight

Line

Tie half-blood knots (see page 10).

Loop to loop knot

Hook length

1. Take all the tackle off your line. Thread a leger weight onto the end of the line. Slide it a little way up.

2. Tie the end of the line to one loop of the swivel. Tie a short piece of line to the swivel's other loop.

3. You can attach a hook length to the short piece of line. Find out about hook lengths on page 11.

Different weights

You use different kinds of weights in different types of water. Some have a hole which you thread the line through and others have a metal loop.

Breakaway weight

Wires grip seabed.

Breakaway weights are good to use in salt water. They have wires that grip the seabed to keep them still when the water is very rough.

Coffin weight

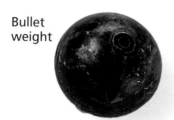

Bullet weight

Bomb weight

Coffin weights have flat sides to stop them from sinking into mud. This shape also keeps them still in rough and flowing water.

Bullet weights are good to use in still and flowing water. In flowing water, the bullet rolls along the bottom of the water.

Bomb weights are the best sort of weight if you want to cast very long distances. You can use them in all kinds of water.

Waiting for a bite

When you are using leger tackle and have cast your line and weight into the water, there is no float to tell you if a fish is biting your bait. Here are two ways to help you tell when it's time to strike.

Quiver tip rod

Tip of rod wiggles when the fish bites.

Pull the line so the bread or silver foil hangs down.

Weight

You can squeeze a ball of bread or silver foil onto the line between the first and second rod rings. When a fish bites the bait, the ball moves up.

Some rods, called quiver tip rods, bend easily near the tip. When a fish bites the bait, it pulls the line and you can see the tip of the rod wiggle around, or quiver.

Overhead casting

Overhead casting lets you throw bait to fish that swim farther from the water's edge. You can cast overhead in any kind of water, as long as there are no trees, bushes or electric wires in the way. For both types of casting shown on these pages, start by following the first three steps in the section on underarm casting on pages 12-13. Only let the line hang a third of the way down your rod, though.

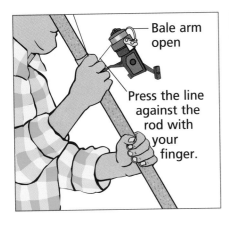

Bale arm open

Press the line against the rod with your finger.

Push this hand away from you.

Pull this hand down.

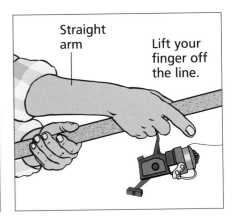

Straight arm

Lift your finger off the line.

1. Swing the rod back a little way, so the line hangs down behind you. Be careful the hook doesn't get tangled in your hair.

2. Quickly jerk the rod forward by pushing away from you with your top hand and pulling down with your bottom hand.

3. When your top arm is straight, lift your finger off the line that is pressed against the rod. This lets more line into the water.

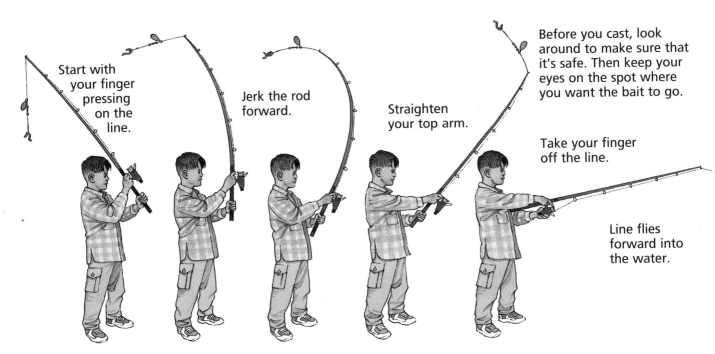

Start with your finger pressing on the line.

Jerk the rod forward.

Straighten your top arm.

Before you cast, look around to make sure that it's safe. Then keep your eyes on the spot where you want the bait to go.

Take your finger off the line.

Line flies forward into the water.

For a link to a website where you can see a clear demonstration of overhead casting, go to **www.usborne-quicklinks.com**

Beach casting

Beach casting is a way of casting overhead. Most sea fish live in deep water, a long way from the beach. Beach casting helps you throw the bait farther to reach these fish. Start with the line the same length as for overhead casting.

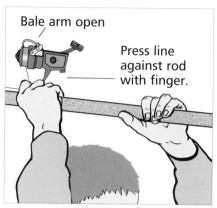

Bale arm open

Press line against rod with finger.

Push this hand away from you.

Pull this hand down.

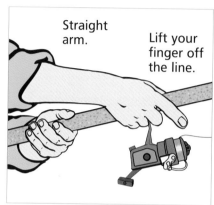

Straight arm.

Lift your finger off the line.

1. Hold the rod directly above your head, as shown here. Stand so one shoulder is pointing in the direction you want to cast.

2. Quickly pull down with your bottom hand and push your top hand forward, over your head until that arm is straight.

3. As soon as your top arm is straight, lift your finger off the line. When the bait hits the water, remember to keep your line tight.

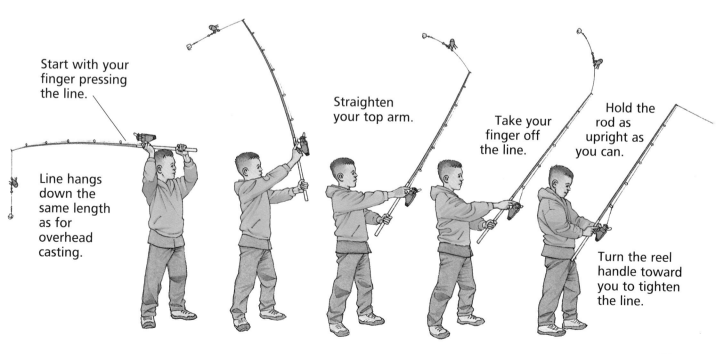

Start with your finger pressing the line.

Line hangs down the same length as for overhead casting.

Straighten your top arm.

Take your finger off the line.

Hold the rod as upright as you can.

Turn the reel handle toward you to tighten the line.

Playing and landing

When a fish bites your bait, you have to get it out of the water. This is called landing. If the fish is small, landing is quite easy. If the fish is bigger, it may try to swim around and you will have to let it get tired before you can land it. This is called playing a fish.

Playing a fish

Big fish can be strong and pull the line hard so that the tip of the rod bends. To stop the fish from pulling you into the water, you can use the reel to give the fish more line so it can swim around. When the fish is tired, the tip of the rod will straighten out.

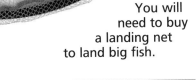

You will need to buy a landing net to land big fish.

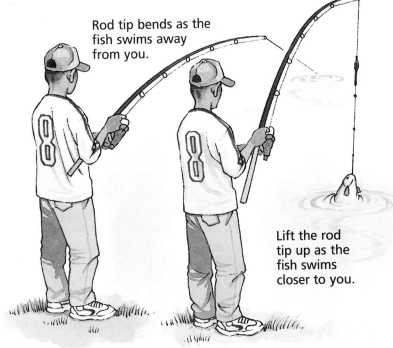

Rod tip bends as the fish swims away from you.

Lift the rod tip up as the fish swims closer to you.

1. As the fish swims away from you and pulls your line, turn the reel handle to let more line into the water.

2. As the fish swims closer to you, lift the rod tip up to tighten the line and stop the fish wriggling off the hook.

Beach landing

When you catch a fish on a beach, turn the reel handle until the fish is partly out of the water. Walk back up the beach and wait for a big wave to wash the fish out of the water.

Landing big fish

Always keep the fish underwater as you bring it to the edge.

Lift rod tip upward.

Keep the rod as upright as possible.

Landing net

1. When the fish is tired, lower the rod tip. Shorten the line by turning the reel handle away from you.

2. When the rod tip is near the water, lift it upward again to pull the fish closer to the water's edge.

3. Ask someone to slide a landing net under the fish, while you hold the rod up to keep the line tight.

Tight line

Landing small fish

4. Turn the reel handle away from you to tighten the line, while your friend lifts the net out of the water.

1. If you have a small fish on your hook, lift the tip of your rod up until the fish is out of the water.

2. Hold the rod handle steadily with one hand. Then you can swing the fish straight into your other hand.

23

Handling fish

When you catch a fish, you have to take the hook out of its mouth. When you have done this, it is a good idea to make a record of the fish in a notebook before you put it back in the water. Always handle fish gently so you do not damage them.

This is a perch. You can find perch in quiet, fresh water.

Always wet your hands before you hold a fish. If it is too big to hold, lay it on some wet grass or a wet cloth.

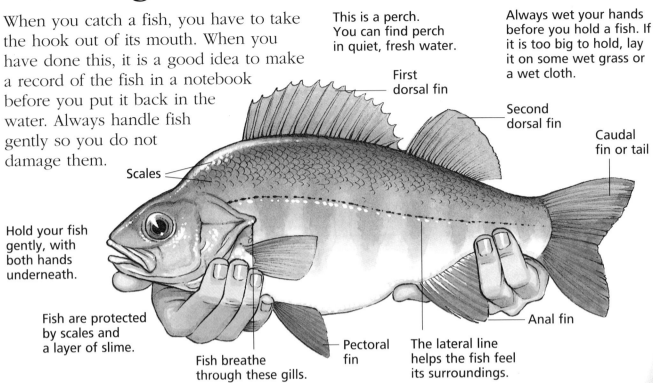

First dorsal fin

Second dorsal fin

Caudal fin or tail

Scales

Hold your fish gently, with both hands underneath.

Fish are protected by scales and a layer of slime.

Fish breathe through these gills.

Pectoral fin

The lateral line helps the fish feel its surroundings.

Anal fin

Unhooking fish

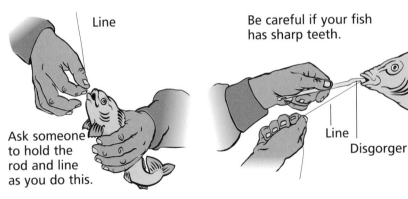

Line

Be careful if your fish has sharp teeth.

Ask someone to hold the rod and line as you do this.

Line

Disgorger

To take a barbless hook out of a small fish's mouth, hold the fish in one hand and the top of the hook in the other. Turn the hook around and slide it out.

If the fish is big, use a tool called a disgorger. Push it onto the line. Slide it down the hook and press it against the bend of the hook to take it out.

Keeping records

Take a notebook with you, so you can keep a record of the fish you catch. Write down details such as the fish's length and weight and any tips that might be useful on your next fishing trip.

Draw a picture of your fish. Look at the shape and the markings.

Use a ruler to measure your fish.

Weighing fish

Weigh each fish you catch so you can compare them. You can buy special weighing scales and net from a tackle store. Here's how to use them.

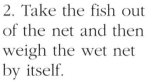

Read the weight here.

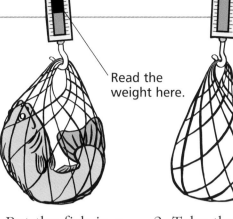

Fish and net = 1.3kg (3lbs)

Wet net = 0.3kg (1lb)

Fish = 1kg (2lbs)

1. Put the fish in a wet net and hang it on the hook. Note down the weight.

2. Take the fish out of the net and then weigh the wet net by itself.

Make a note of when and where you caught your fish.

3. Subtract the weight of the wet net to find the weight of the fish.

Note down what the weather was like and if the water was still or fast-flowing, salt water or fresh water.

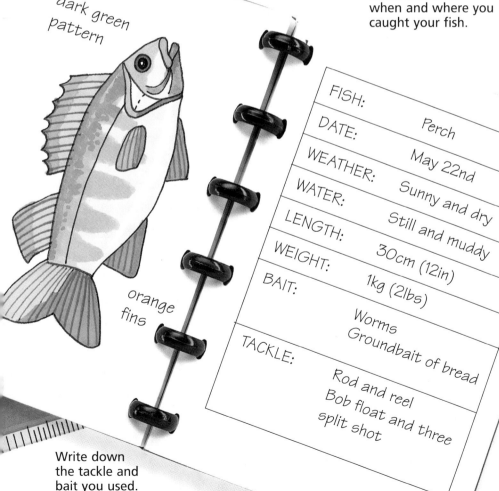

dark green pattern

orange fins

FISH: Perch

DATE: May 22nd

WEATHER: Sunny and dry

WATER: Still and muddy

LENGTH: 30cm (12in)

WEIGHT: 1kg (2lbs)

BAIT: Worms
Groundbait of bread

TACKLE: Rod and reel
Bob float and three
split shot

Write down the tackle and bait you used.

Try to find out the name of your fish. Look at pages 28 and 29 of this book or ask an angler with more experience.

Putting fish back

Put your fish back in the water near the place where you caught it. Hold the fish just under the water for a few seconds, then release it and let it swim away.

Baits

Here are some of the baits anglers use to attract fish. Different fish like different baits, so it is a good idea to try out a few. You can think up some of your own baits too and make a note of the ones which are the most successful.

Corn

Sweet foods such as marshmallows and jellybeans

Cubes of cheese

Cooked pasta shapes

You can make bread balls by soaking stale bread in water and rolling it into balls.

Small pieces of bread

Putting bait on a hook

To make sure the hook goes into the fish's mouth, push it all the way through the bait so you can see the point on the other side. You can put one or more pieces of bait on one hook. Be careful not to hurt yourself on the hook.

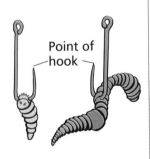

Point of hook

Push the hook through the end of a maggot and through the middle of a worm.

Worms make excellent bait. You can dig up different types in soil and sand.

Maggots are the grubs of flies. You can buy them in tackle stores. If you keep them cool, they last about a week.

For a link to a website where you can play a fun game called Fish Food, go to www.usborne-quicklinks.com

Flies and lures

Some anglers attach flies or lures to their lines instead of hooks and bait. Flies look like the living insects and lures look like the small fish that some fish feed on. They are more difficult to use than ordinary bait. You will need to buy special tackle and do lots of practice if you want to use them.

Groundbait

You can attract fish to the area where you are fishing by throwing a handful of bait, called groundbait, into the water. You can try out any kind of bait as groundbait. Don't use too much, or the fish will not want to eat the bait on the hook.

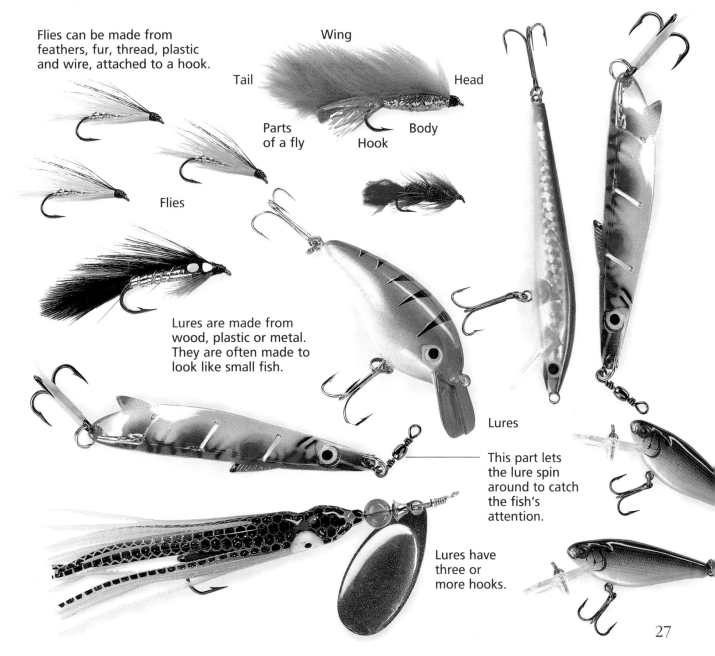

Flies can be made from feathers, fur, thread, plastic and wire, attached to a hook.

Wing

Tail

Head

Parts of a fly

Body

Hook

Flies

Lures are made from wood, plastic or metal. They are often made to look like small fish.

Lures

This part lets the lure spin around to catch the fish's attention.

Lures have three or more hooks.

Freshwater and saltwater fish

These pages show just some of the many fish that live around the world and the types of water where you can find them.

Freshwater fish

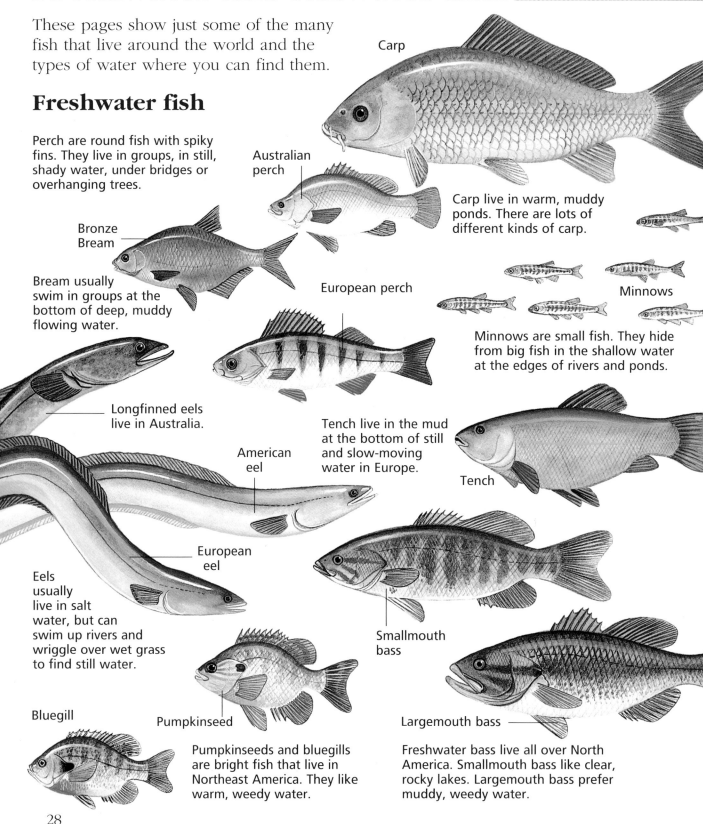

Perch are round fish with spiky fins. They live in groups, in still, shady water, under bridges or overhanging trees.

Carp

Australian perch

Bronze Bream

Bream usually swim in groups at the bottom of deep, muddy flowing water.

European perch

Carp live in warm, muddy ponds. There are lots of different kinds of carp.

Minnows

Minnows are small fish. They hide from big fish in the shallow water at the edges of rivers and ponds.

Longfinned eels live in Australia.

American eel

Tench live in the mud at the bottom of still and slow-moving water in Europe.

Tench

European eel

Eels usually live in salt water, but can swim up rivers and wriggle over wet grass to find still water.

Smallmouth bass

Bluegill

Pumpkinseed

Largemouth bass

Pumpkinseeds and bluegills are bright fish that live in Northeast America. They like warm, weedy water.

Freshwater bass live all over North America. Smallmouth bass like clear, rocky lakes. Largemouth bass prefer muddy, weedy water.

*For a link to a website where you can watch an amazing video clip of a salmon swimming upstream, go to **www.usborne-quicklinks.com***

Saltwater fish

Pomano live in warm water, in all parts of the world. This largespot pomano lives around Africa, India and Australia.

Largespot pomano

Mackerel are fast fish. They swim in groups near the surface of the water.

Mackerel

Mullet

Mullet are silver fish. They often swim near moored boats, looking for food.

Plaice

Plaice are flat fish with orange spots. They like to live on the sea-bed, half-buried in the sand.

Ballan wrasse are usually reddish brown with silver spots. They live among rocks and weeds and often swim close to the shore.

Ballan wrasse

Saltwater eels do not have scales. They can grow to enormous sizes.

Surfperch

Surfperch live at the bottom of the water off the West Coast of North America.

Conger eel

Cod usually live in cold, deep water, but sometimes you can find them close to the shore.

Moray eel

Red drum

Red drum have a dark spot near the tail. They live in North America and like to swim close to the bottom of the water.

Cod

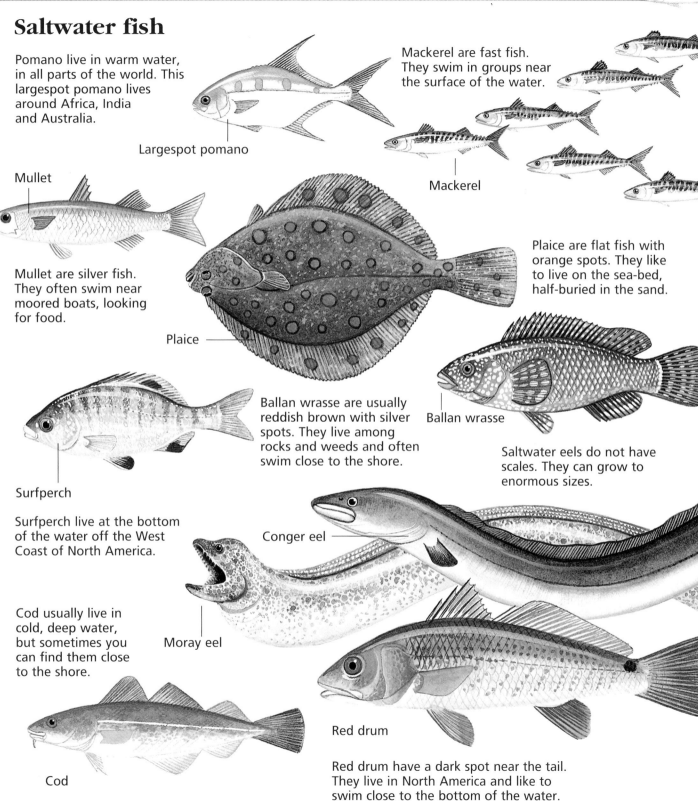

The countryside

For a link to a website where you can find out how you can help protect fish and play a fun game, go to *www.usborne-quicklinks.com*

To avoid causing damage to the countryside, always follow the angling code shown on this page. Look out for any signs of damage to the countryside, such as polluted water, and report them to a fishing club or a fishing organization.

Fishing clubs

Fishing clubs often own stretches of water where you can fish. It costs very little to join and you can learn lots of tips from other anglers. You can find out where your nearest fishing club is from one of the organizations on the opposite page.

Polluted water

Water that is very dirty, or polluted, harms fish. You should never fish in polluted water and always tell a fishing club about it. Here are some signs of pollution.

Waste

Smelly water

Sewage

Dirty foam

Oily water

Dead fish

Angling code

• Always take your litter home with you. Tackle such as fishing line and hooks can be very harmful to wildlife if you leave it lying around.

• Make sure you always close any gates behind you.

• Move around quietly so you do not disturb wildlife.

• Try not to disturb other anglers when they are fishing.

• Be careful not to damage trees and bushes or the edge of the water.

• Only buy weights that will not harm wildlife. Lead weights should not be used in fresh water because they may poison water birds.

Glossary

Here are some of the fishing words you can find in this book.

Bait - little pieces of food you put on your hook to make fish want to bite it.

A bite - when a fish bites your bait.

Casting - using a rod to throw your line, hook and bait into the water.

Closed season - time of year when fish lay eggs. You are not allowed to fish during the closed season.

Fishing permit - piece of paper that allows you to fish in certain places.

Float fishing - using floats to help you catch fish that swim near the surface of the water.

Fresh water - the water in rivers, streams, canals, lakes and ponds.

Groundbait - small pieces of bait you throw into the water to attract fish to the area where you are fishing.

Hook length - short piece of line with a hook tied to one end and a loop at the other which you can attach to the main line.

Landing - bringing the fish onto the land.

Leger fishing - using weights to help you catch fish that swim near the bottom of the water and far away from the water's edge.

Maggots - grubs of flies that you can use as bait.

Playing - letting a fish swim around to get tired before you bring it to the edge of the water.

Pollution - when water is very dirty. It can harm fish.

Salt water - the water in seas and oceans.

Setting the float - making sure the float is in the right position in the water.

Striking - lifting the tip of your rod up to make sure the hook goes into the fish's mouth, when you feel the fish bite your bait.

Tackle - the equipment you need to go fishing.

Fishing organizations

National Federation of Anglers
Halliday House
Eggington Junction
Derbyshire
DE65 6GU
UK

Future Fisherman Foundation
Suite 200
1033 North Fairfax Street
Alexandria, VA 22314
USA

Recfish Australia
PO Box 854
Dickson
ACT 2602
Australia

Index

With thanks to:
Chris Vaughan, Charlie Marha, Bob Sharp and John Collins of OkieBug.

First published in 1998 by Usborne Publishing Ltd, 83–85 Saffron Hill, London EC1N 8RT, England. www.usborne.com Copyright © 2003, 1998 Usborne Publishing Ltd. First published in America in1999. This edition published in America in 2004. The name Usborne and the devices ♀ ⊕ are Trade Marks of Usborne Publishing Ltd. All rights reserved. No part of this publication may be reproduced, stored in a retrieval system, or transmitted in any form or by any means, electronic, mechanical, photocopying, recording or otherwise, without the prior permission of the publisher. UE. Printed in Belgium.

Usborne Publishing is not responsible, and does not accept liability, for the availability or content of any website other than its own, or for any exposure to harmful, offensive, or inaccurate material which may appear on the Web. Usborne Publishing will have no liability for any damage or loss caused by viruses that may be downloaded as a result of browsing the sites we recommend.